Vagrant Whispers

A compilation of short stories and
a sprinkle of poetry by

JOANNA FOLEY

Printed in the United States
Edited by Keidi Keating
Layout by Rochelle Mensidor

ISBN: 979-8-9897121-3-7

Index.

Nature, unnatural contains;

Man of the Sea

Season of Regret

An Alien for Tea

Dragon Wings

Winter's Children

Humanity contains;

Saint of Foresight

Bookend

The Comedian

The Parade

Vengeance

Haunting contains;

The Fallout

Suzannah

Life in Stasis

Shopping Centre

Muttropolis contains;

Bottlecap

Dear Mam

A Walk in Winter

Westietude

Introduction.

Hello! My name is Joanna, and I will be your
tour guide on this magical adventure.

The following collection is a blend of fantasy, horror,
romance, humour, and forty-million other things mixed
in, so I hope there's something here for everyone.

I live in Mallow, Co Cork which is in the South of Ireland with my husband, Eoin. I love to cross stitch and play video games, as well as collect and restore vintage toys and dolls.

As well as short stories and flash-fiction, I have written my first novel, Alderwood House, which I hope to have published soon. You can follow me as Foleysfables on social media for any upcoming news. I also have the first two novels of a fantasy series, Other Earth, done, so I've been a busy writing bee!

I wanted to do something fun with some of the shorter pieces, and this piece of work you hold in your hand is the result of that wish. I really hope you will enjoy it.

Nature, Unnatural.

Man of the Sea

A flash of lightning, his tail an electrical dash of violent blue through placid waters. Loneliness presses in around him amid the ocean's depths, and he heeds the internal call of the terrestrial world, tiring of seaweed and tedious fish for company.

Reaching the line of strand that is familiar, he crawls from the water on strong arms, panting in the human worlds' air with rusty huffs. He rests for a moment amidst the suds of the late evening tide, recalling the taste of the seaside zephyr. His tail transforms as he pulls himself further inland. Coarse, damp sand sticks to him. Vibrant colour becomes muted from a lively blue to a peachy hue, one muscular limb splitting painfully in two. Bones rending, establishing joints as his human legs form.

He waits for the pain to subside and stands, his breathing easier now. A cold breeze refreshes his skin; the smell of the salt and the wind is reassuring. The wind worn cabin beyond the sand dunes is his destination once he has both symbolically and literally found his feet.

The last remnants of light from the setting sun glimmer through the tattered remains of a lace curtain, hung decades earlier by unknown hands over its one tiny window. It is nearly dark when he enters.

His toes splay over floorboards that creak as he crosses the room. He reaches up for his neatly pressed suit that hangs waiting, suspended above what once may have been a dressmaker's studio.

An old sewing machine sits on the workbench, rusting in its retirement. Dressed and drab, he is ready to enter the human world once more. As usual, he will blend in with the loud, unpredictable beings undetected. In time, he will find a lady to share the joys of the dry world with before the ocean's inevitable call sends him back to it once more.

Season of Regret

*(Previously shortlisted and published in the
From The Well short story Anthology 2022)*

She swallowed down her remorse, flashing him one last smile that was too bright to be real. Grey streaks dappled through his unkempt mane as the winds tousled it, roiling his jacket around him as he winked at her, then turned to the road. Nothing changed with him; he was hot, then cold. Warm then gone.

It always happened the same way. She would make a quiet, observant entrance and his eyes would find hers from across the room as soon as she arrived. He would be irritated with her if she was late, but he was not malicious and soon he would be at her side, helping her to prepare for her upcoming shift. Their attraction would be powerful, their time together fleeting. They would fill their days working together or if they were lucky, *weeks* until he would have to pack up his life and move on.

A very small part of her hated their dalliances, how sometimes the way he held on to her made her feel like the very tips of her fingers would burn off from the intensity of his touch. Yet she loved how most of the time they moved together with faultless accord. They were an odd couple; she a pale whip of a thing in her simple white dress and he a rugged wall, dressed in tattered denim and leather.

Though they were the same age, he had seen more hardship than her and the fine lines of his weather-tanned skin showed it.

She bit at her lip then turned, unwilling to watch him walk any further away. She hoped he might roll into town on an unexpected whim, like a powerful storm-cloud that would stir her around and mess with her plans, though he never meant to. It was his nature to be so wayward.

They would not get to spend any real length of time together like this for months, until this schedule of theirs repeated itself. Before it was time for him to leave, he would say to her with a tender kiss on the tip of her nose that she unlocked things that lay buried deep within him, and then she would smile and tell him that she would miss him.

"I love you, Spring!" He called to her, and she turned again, overwhelmed by his smile before he bowed into the wind and was gone.

"I love you too, Winter…" She whispered as a lone tear escaped her eye. Regret burned deep down in her chest, for she could never find the courage to share those weighty words with him aloud.

Alien for Tea

One night I encountered an alien,
Thought it polite to offer some tea.
I, wrapped in robes; she with her probes,
What a strange sight were we!

"Why do you pour cold liquid into
that juice that is meant to be hot?
Why not cook it to the right temperature,
Then this ritual be needed not?"

I shook my head at the alien,
As I offered a hobnob or two,
"Everyone drinks their tea differently,
You'll have to find what works for you!"

Dragon Wings

The sky looms around me as I am enveloped by cotton-damp clouds. Up here, it is moist; the air a tepid cocoon.

When I stole the dragon's wings, I did not know of the curse that niggled within their flaky DNA. When those fleshy limbs were joined to me, how could I know that instead of giving me the world, they would take it from me?

My mind wavers as I glide through the cirrus tufts of white. I drift down towards the nearest mountain peak, only partially aware of my body's motions.

In killing the beast and taking its wings, I have unleashed the cruellest type of revenge. Now, I become the very creature I killed, doomed to a world of mindless plunder and flight until the next Knight with notions of power strikes an iron through my breast.

I smell meat... I smell children.

Winter's Children

Nettle soup for my children. For me, old water boiled over the faltering embers of a since-dead fire. I grow too weak to look for kindling, even slender twigs of deadwood would suffice, but I cannot go.

The children lie huddled by my sides, sharing what little comfort can be sourced from the glowing remnants of life within the embers. These cinders broil, bright on their rocky bed as gales of wind disturb their slumber, then dull down to sleep once more.

The children grow still.

This rocky ground we lie on is flaked over with frost, crunchy and fragile, yet strong enough to make us ill, to keep us still.

My fingers burn, purple and old before their time. Like talons, they grasp my shawl tight around us to shelter from raindrops, heavy and cruel. The sun begins to rise, and our quarry takes on a bluish tint. No heat to be found, even in the unfurling fingertips of the waking sun. Wet and cold I lie, beyond shivers, with my silent infants. They are winter's children now and will never know the gentle warmth of spring.

My vision is clouded by unfallen tears, and a darkness takes hold of my sight. A cold unlike winter's cruel pinch spreads from my toes, up and along until I too, am gone.

Humanity

Saint of Foresight

(Previously shortlisted and published in
From The Well short story Anthology 2020)

My name is Clover.

I'm that girl you read about in newspapers, the one that thousands of people from across the world are calling a 'Saint of Foresight.' Even my name screams mythology.

I'm not a saint, I'm no devil either. I'm a fifteen-year-old girl from the west of Ireland. I used to go to school, go shopping; I used to worry about boys. Just like my friends. That was until word got out about my 'gift.'

It's hard to describe what it's like to touch a person and see when they will die. Every detail comes to me in slow, excruciating clarity. Now, people from all over flock to our door to find out when it will be their time to die, to see if it can be changed. Or stalled.

My stepfather, Jim, who rejected my presence until this came out, saw money signs around me right away. It didn't take him long to get a team of lawyers to surround the family, like vultures to a carcass. My mother, as usual, went along with whatever he decided.

I'm not allowed to see my friends anymore. I can't leave the house. The small, two-bedroomed terrace home I grew up in has become my prison.

A lot of people get angry when they learn about their death day. I mean, it's usually only high-end business folk that can afford to visit me, thanks to good old Jim. They want to keep on earning big bucks forever.

I'd never seen my own death day. Not until the meeting this morning, when a fat Polish diplomat shook my hand. The rings on his fingers pinched at my skin, and when I pulled my hand away, there it was.

My future.

I started to laugh. It got worse as the big buffoons' cheeks turned red, then purple. Boy, he was angry, but I just couldn't help myself. Jim smoothed him over, with the promise of another meeting this afternoon once I had rested. The slap he flung across my face burned, but still I laughed. My mother flew at him, and while the two of them were locked together in verbal combat, I retreated to my room.

A loud boom from downstairs rattled the picture frames on my bedroom wall. At this point, I wasn't sure if I was laughing or crying. I think it was both. Jim is hollering my name as he stomps his way up our narrow stairs.

I wave down at the crowd of people below that have come in the hopes of catching a glimpse of me. What will happen next might be the beginning of the best journey I will ever go on. The door clatters against the wall behind me as Jim kicks it open.

There is no changing destiny.

He is screaming at me, but all I can hear is the cheerful singing from those outside. I concentrate on their smiles, on their excitement as the shooter hiding in the crowd below raises his gun and pulls the trigger.

My chest explodes.

Finally, I am free.

The Bookend

A dog-shaped bookend sat deserted on a shelf. Its wooden legs hung over the edge as if it were contemplating a leap to its death. The second-hand shop was filled with a musty smell that the old garments of clothing would hold deep in their fibres. Chloe retreated to the back of the shop while her nana chatted with her friend behind the counter. The toys and books were kept at the back, and they held a much more pleasant scent.

She flicked through the children's books, mindless of their contents, until she spotted the little wooden dog keeping vigil at his end of the bookshelves. She searched for a companion, finding none. She picked it up and traced her nail-painted fingers along it, admiring the human-like pose it sat in, with its legs dangling from a seated position.

She traced them over its sad face, over the delicate features carved onto its light, wooden body. Perfect black dots of paint sat on a coat of white, which she recognised. It was supposed to be a dalmatian. She sidled up to her nana at the counter and placed her treasure with care into the mishmash of random balls of wool that nana was buying. Her grandmother smiled down at her with over-white false teeth, and the skin in the corners of her eyes crinkled in crow-legged lines.

When they got home, Chloe retrieved the little statue, and darted to her bedroom. She owned many books and toys, which were lined up on mis-matched shelves, that too were rescued from different thrift shops. She placed the little dog up on the shelf, next to one that was identical to it. She had found her bookend a twin, and now her shelf of fairy-tale stories and treasures felt complete.

Two little wooden dalmatians sat side-by-side, their feet dangling over the edge of the shelf they sat on, as if cooling down near the edge of a lake on a hot summer day.

Two little dalmatian bookends, a pair, once more.

The Comedian

The crowd babbles boisterously,
As the seats fill up one by one.
A hush falls as the announcements start,
And we know this will be fun!

The Comedian crashes his way onstage,
With a crazy, prancing gait.
He fills the stage with movement and,
The crowd just cannot wait.

His jokes begin and peals of laughter,
Fill up the crowded room.
The Comedian's voice echoes through,
The mic with an electronic boom.

Tears streaming down our faces,
"It all ends too soon!" We cry!
We clap and cheer and shout, "Encore!"
And of course, he does oblige.

I wonder about The Comedian though,
When the stage lights all go dim.
The crowd goes home, the show is done—
Who is left to accompany him?

The Parade

I knew today would be a big selling day for us, with the famous parade held in our town this year. My wife and I have been planning this stall for months, painting bright banners and experimenting with all sorts of colourful waxes to coat our cheeses with. The brighter, the better!

The best-selling cheeses for us are the rainbow-coloured wheels. They take the longest time to create as the cheese had to be dipped in different coloured waxes to achieve the variegated effect. It's paid off though, we can't sell them fast enough!

I have a great view of the parade as it passes, though I'm almost deafened by the excited shrieks of enthusiastic parade folk and the loud techno music. Every so often the wife will clear off the tabletop of our stall as it gets covered in shards of bright paper confetti.

The parade is really something, in between serving customers I try to take it all in. The showy flash of colours, the rich smell of spices and popcorn from nearby stalls, and the sounds. Life on the farm is quiet, peaceful compared to this exuberant display.

Handing over a bright pink Edam to a rosy-haired lady with a nose ring, his eyes meet mine through the crowd. His gaze holds mine like a silent bubble between us within the madness.

Alberto… He is parading along the street in front of his group of carnival people with a costume that shows off every sturdy muscle. A glittery strap of cloth that leaves very little to the imagination.

A colossal plume of ostrich feathers splays out behind him as he saunters through the main street, twirling in my direction with exotic enthusiasm once he has seen me. He winks, blowing me a knowing kiss through the unsuspecting crowd before he is gone in the flurry of the parade. My heart thumps intense beats within my chest, they sound so loud in my ears that it roars over any noise that the parade makes.

I look over at my wife. She is a beautiful, kind woman that is ever polite. She smiles as she handles a customer's change and I can only just manage to swallow down my own saliva. A sense of cold, shivering guilt washes over me.

I am fond of her, truly I am. I wonder as the next rainbow-dressed customer decides on their cheese of choice, just how much longer I can keep this from her.

My heart belongs to Alberto.

Vengeance

(Winning piece in an international short story competition, published in The Snake Pit anthology 2023 in the U.S.A.)

The declaration of their engagement at last night's banquet made the meat in my mouth sour over, like bile. I forced the mouthful down and obliged my lips to curve into an expected smile. Artos, my older brother stood, arrogant as ever at the head of the table, gazing into the lavender eyes of Princess Ketall.

Ketall is the love of my lifetime.

When her family would visit our palace each summer, it was I that she would sit with and read stories to in the gardens from her books of fairy-tale. It was I that she explored the vast catacombs under the fortress with, citing tales of legends long past and fables of terrific ghosts. It was I who plucked her into my arms and ran with, when the Quaritites attacked the city.

Yet, there my brother stood, winding a serpentine arm around her waist as she stood at his side. She was to be his bride. His Queen.

I won't allow it.

My brother is a foolish man. He is more concerned with hunting boar through the forests with his friends than with the kingdom he will one day inherit from my father. No, he cannot adore her in the manner which I do.

I cannot outright kill him, for that would lose me the respect of Ketall and gain me a noose about the neck. And so, I stole her heart and fused it with my own.

It was challenging, the science of it beyond explanation to any mere dullard. Yet, I understood the makings of the spell for all of the lore was there, in the forbidden rooms beyond the catacombs. In the rooms that Ketall and I discovered and explored many years before.

They will never suspect me of foul play, for I have kept my adequacy as a mage well hidden. In these dark times, it would be foolish to claim oneself as Blessed. I keep but one tome in my private quarters which is written in the ancient tongue. It is the one possession I treasure most for, in it are the formulas of many dark and powerful spells of old.

A slip of her hair was easy to procure, as was a vial of her blood. Her handmaid is a greedy sort, and at the promise of coppers she was glad to acquire them from the sleeping Princess. People truly are *disgusting*. Many more ingredients made up the potion that I drank. Once it was consumed, several hours of pain vibrated through my bones during a night I feared would be never-ending.

This morrow as the Cockerel began his tune, as the hints of orange slipped across the sky like a slit of blood from a wound, the spell began its work. The wooden bowl I filled with goose feathers at the end of my bed began to glow. I crept down along my bunk to observe, as sweat from exhaustion beaded around my eyes and dripped from my forehead.

Fragments of red crystal sprouted and sparkled inside, as long glasslike shards of the Princesses heart formed within. It took but a moment before eight glorious glittering gemstones lay gleaming in their downy bed.

Of course, nobody would question the Princesses' sudden bout of illness as anything else other than bad wine or meat from yesterday's feast. She will suffer as I did, until the sun retreats this night.

Now the most difficult part of the process can begin. I sit at the end of my bed, naked as the day I first entered the world. I gather myself for a breath and let my thoughts simmer on my brother. Anger fuels me once more. I clench my shaking fists together over my breast until my breathing slows, and I become calm. My hand trembles as I reach towards the bowl for one of the Heartshards. The sting of its ice cool touch betrays its terrible purpose.

I keep still, and on a deep inward breath I press the sharpest end of the crystal into the flesh of my upper body. I bite back a cry as I twist it in between the ribs that cage my organs, yet a screech betrays my lips as it pierces my own beating heart. The agony drops me into a dark slumber from which I rouse much later. I see no blood, just the flat end of the crystal, which is visible and flush with my skin.

Seven more times I repeat this dreadful task. Melting the long red slivers through the flesh of my chest until they stake my heart like the claws of a bear. The sun is retreating as the day comes to an end.

I stand and observe myself in the cracked mirror by my wash basin. Eight red jewels glisten in my skin, that betray the whereabouts of the thundering heart within. Ketall's heart is now welded to my own. She will seek me out without understanding the reasoning behind it, for a soul needs to be close to its heart to be complete.

In a week or perhaps two, it is *I*, Terane, who shall stand at the head of the feast table with my beloved Ketall by my side.

She is mine.

Haunting

The Fallout

I don't wish to set this world on fire, but I would be glad to watch it burn again.

I lie still on my makeshift bed in this dilapidated shack, listening to the sounds of the creature crawling across the roof overhead. I can hear its sharp claws screeching across the roofs rusted metal as it searches for its prey. And I can just about make out the low chittering sounds it makes to communicate to others of its kind. It hasn't discovered me, yet. I close my eyes and hold my breath as the terror grips my chest, burning me within.

This world was a normal place, once. People lived, worked, loved, and argued. It was a predictable, yet safe existence. Until the Third Great War started, that is. The rich countries started using Bio-nuclear weapons against each other, because bullets and bombs just weren't enough to help them decide on a winner.

That was the beginning of the end of the world, orchestrated by finely suited fat-cats in their fancy offices. Men and women that needed only to press an icon on a screen to ruin millions of lives.

Their expensive new weapons didn't *just* kill people, fry them in their tracks as they shattered the world around them. No, they arrived carrying an extra surprise, shocking even to its creators. A surprise that first manifested in the surviving population weeks after the bombs had dropped, once the city-wide fires started to die down and the dust began to clear over the wealth of rubble where looming cities once stood.

Anyone lucky enough to survive the blazing chaos all around, as well as the looters and the crazy people with guns might soon get another shudder to the system as they started to feel themselves change. They were forced to endure the unquenchable cravings that overcame them. It happened to my mother. We were wondering why she itched so bad one night, only to see her skin turning shiny and black where she scratched at it. I can still hear the pitch of her screams as the extra appendages burst from the skin of her back.

You still had your own mind, they said, as your body was mutating into whatever abominations this war had turned people into. After a time, you wouldn't even be able to speak anymore. What was left of your human face would be encased under a newer, more frightening visage. Even your thoughts would turn feral, and then, you were one of them.

Shit. There are two of them up there now, shrilling and hissing at each other. They sound excited about something. Please don't be me they sense, please don't be me…

They are gone in a deafening clash of metal and speed, and I hear a harsh yelping sound off to the left of my temporary haven. They've found one of the stray dogs that roam around here. Poor bastard. The noises abate as their victim is hauled off into the night to become their next feast. I let out the painful breath that I've been holding in with a burning whoosh, glad that it wasn't me they found.

I need to keep moving around this burned-out husk of a world. Staying in one place for too long would be like putting up a giant neon sign that screams, 'I'm here. Come and eat me!' The daytime isn't as bad because they don't seem to be active during sun-up. That's when I get most of my exploring done.

I have this huge fold-out map of the city in my rucksack that I found on one of my foraging trips. In the mornings, I travel that bit further along where it marks the road forward. I'll stay in a new area until I've used up most of the things I can find there, like canned foods and bottled water.

It sucks, because in a world like this you stink to high hell and your hair itches all the time. I cut mine short, so the fleas have nowhere to lodge themselves. And a creature can't snag you by the hair in a darkened alleyway if you have none.

I sometimes wonder what the tutor of my beauticians' course at college would say to me as I hack away at my locks. Then I remember that she's probably dead by now, and I trim it all the faster.

Now that it is quiet outside, I sit up in my sleeping bag to do a mental checklist of my belongings, like I do every night. There's my rucksack with my spare clothes, my scissors for my hair, a small flashlight for emergencies and half of a packet of only-somewhat-mouldy biscuits. On the dirt floor next to me is a pack of tealights and two boxes of matches that I found this morning inside of a shed, three bottles of clean water and two cans of peaches.

One of the small tealights is the only bit of light I'll allow in the room. It's all I can afford to burn, with those six-legged aberrations lurking around. There have been more and more of them skulking about the area over the last week. It's too dangerous to stay here any longer. Time to move on. I get to packing everything up into my bag as quiet as I can before pulling out my map to plan the next part of my journey.

Nobody tells you just how tiring the apocalypse is going to be. It's not so much the constant fear for your safety or the running from place to place, although that certainly takes its toll on a person's mind. It's beyond stressful. Deep in the night you think that everything is finally alright. *I'm inside now, safe and sound, and I can get some rest.*

That's when the utter boredom of it all sets in. The lethargy of this whole thing is the real killer. Long hours spent encased in whatever place you've called home for the night with not much to do. Waiting for the screeching and the hissing to start up outside, as it always does. Books don't survive well from a worldwide scorching, and without any electricity you can forget about getting that perfect high-score playing Pacman.

When I'm bored at night I often get lost in thought, thinking back on how this all happened. And before I know it, I've scratched my arms raw without even noticing. Damned fleas are getting to be a real pest. That's what I tell myself at least, as I roll my sleeping bag up and attach it to my backpack, ready for the days adventuring ahead.

The less I let myself dwell on the little black flakes of skin showing up where I've been scratching, the easier my day is to get through. I hike my rucksack over my shoulder and peep out through a small hole in the door, made in the past with a stray bullet. The sun is up.

Time to move on.

Suzannah

My aversion to her had been immediate, a sensation so deeply rooted within that the mere sight of her made me feel queasy. She had been a gift from Aunt Leanna, one of those relatives that one sees perhaps once a year, when they return from whichever part of the world they have been exploring on their current whim for adventure.

The box holding her had been beautiful, an ornate wooden affair which when opened had contained something wrapped in delicate sheets of pink tissue paper. My young-self had been eager for the possibilities within until I teased the paper away and found myself staring into her dead, glass eyes.

A porcelain doll. I had forced a delighted smile on my face, and I thanked Aunt Leanna profusely. Knowing that the crinkles in the corner of her eyes as she beamed meant that she was pleased with my response. My heart, however, seemed to fall low in my chest as I beheld my new treasure. I gazed into the cold green eyes then took in its brash painted lips.

I remember thinking, *is it the little rows of perfect teeth that bothered me?* Her toothy grin reminded me of a predator, like the sharks you see in documentaries, eyes cold and mouth ajar as they move in for the kill.

Aunt Leanna left that evening and the doll had been consigned, box and all, to the back of my wardrobe where I did not have to look at it. My mother's attempts to persuade me to display it with my other toys on the shelves were futile. She could not comprehend my dislike towards it any more than I could have put the feeling into words.

Within days I had all but forgotten about the doll, field trips at school and play dates with friends took precedent, as they do. Binky, the families Yorkshire terrier went missing at the end of that week, which had the family fraught with worry. My mother's scream the following morning as she entered my wardrobe to hang my freshly laundered dresses brought the whole household upstairs in a rush before she shut the door. She ushered my brother and I back down the stairs while giving teary-eyed looks to my father, telling him without words to go and see for himself.

I never found out exactly what happened that day, but the fabric mat inside my wardrobe had been removed and a fresh mound of dirt at the bottom of the back yard told me what I needed to know. My parents never quite looked at me the same after that. And though nothing had been said, I knew that they thought I had done something dreadful to Binky.

Poor Binky, my closest companion, now lay a dirty secret buried at the bottom of the yard while my parents and brother began to speak carefully around me. Often sharing glances with each other after each sentence I spoke.

Had things ended there, life might have eventually moved on, but no—that was not to be. Suzannah, the name given to the infernal doll with her black ringlets by my Aunt, started to turn up in different areas of the house. Though nobody had placed her there. I would wake to the sound of a child's laughter to find her lying across the duvet at the end of my bed, those rose red lips of hers seeming bloodstained in the hazy light of the new morning.

I would shove her into her box and to the back of the wardrobe, until she embarked on her next escapade around the house. My brothers pet hamster soon died under "suspicious" circumstances. Suzannah had been sitting alongside the unfortunate creature's cage, gleaming with her usual smile. My mother had pulled me into his room, shouting and pointing at the deceased rodent and the doll, screaming at me that I needed to stop this crazy behaviour.

I remember looking up at her as she twisted my arm, my response was that it was the dolls doing. Which caused tears to spill over her eyelids and onto my pink t-shirt as she turned and pushed me back towards my own bedroom. I was told to stay and think about what I had done.

The next morning, after a feverish night's sleep, I had woken up to a quiet house, eerie and still as I padded my way barefoot through the hall to my parent's bedroom. The sight that met me there produced a dagger of fear from my throat down to my toes. My parents lay askew in bed, sheets spreading a slow pattern of blood, which soaked down from the deep wounds in their throats.

Perhaps it was my screaming that alerted the neighbours. Perhaps it was the still form of my brother, who had made it as far as the front garden before blood loss had forced him to drop where he stood, dead in the grass. Susannah lay in the bedroom doorway. Pristine as always and though I protested to the policemen that bundled me away in an unmarked vehicle, they brought her along with me. Thinking her a valued companion of mine.

I didn't answer their questions, remained silent as her gaze bored into mine from my lap. Why was there blood all over my clothing? Why was there a kitchen knife found in my bed? I could not answer. She forbade it with her malevolent glare, and all that I could do was smile down at her as I finally understood.

She was not the plaything in our relationship, I was.

It has been years since all of that has happened, and I remain silent with only Suzannah for company in my simple, clean cell at the end of the ward. I would spend time talking to the others that live here, but I know that Susannah is jealous and would kill them. So I choose to sit by the window of my room each day with her, coiling her now ratty curls around my fingers as we waste the days away, together.

I have always hated her, and yet, she is such a vast part of me that I fear I also love her.

Life in Stasis

It was a surprise to the public when renowned sculptor, Julio Marquez, announced his next exhibition to the world via a short blurb on his blog.

Two years prior to this announcement, he had lost most of his left arm in a freak accident, when a large block on top of the local church crumbled and fell. Crushing him. He had spent months in the hospital recovering, but there had been no way to save his arm. It was thought that he would never sculpt again.

The blurb read: *Introducing a new exhibition on life in stasis, featuring the realism of true form encapsulated in resin.*

Simple. Effective. The tickets for the opening event sold out within an hour, and many were resold online to high-paying bidders from the upper crust of the socialite scene.

When the evening came, the crowd sat in comfortable padded seats across from a thick, dark curtain that had been set up across the local gallery's main floor. Julio stood before the group. It was detailed in later newspaper articles that he looked small, a spectre of his earlier self with scruffy clothes and long, untamed hair.

There had been much speculation on the possible theme of his new work. Wood and stone were his previous materials of choice, but these had been discounted. How could a man with one arm wield and work with such heavy materials?

His speech had been short, more of a semi-coherent ramble about life-after-death, than anything substantial. The curtain was pulled aside, and for a moment, silence filled the room before the crowd was on their feet, taking in the exhibition with hushed whispers and sober nods.

When photographs of the event were published online, there was both admiration and uproar. How did he do it? How could an artist known for his simplistic style create such vivid, life-like recreations of humanity, and with what materials?

He remained silent on the matter, simply stating whenever asked, that he had encapsulated life in resin. A detailed article had been made and submitted to Wikipedia, which read in part: *The exhibit consisted of ten pieces, each similar in style while showcasing differences in humanity. Ranging from age to race. Each mannequin, for better term of description, was presented nude, without addition of hair. Each mannequin held an expression of calm, almost sleepiness, which was encased in a thick cast of clear resin.*

The idea of life trapped or halted in time came to many when taking in these pieces, but the question on most people's minds continued to elude them. How could the young man have created such detailed portrayals of humanity, with delicate raised veins, wrinkles, and blotchy blood vessels, in such a short time and with limited capacity?

As we now know, these questions were pertinent. It took one week for the first reports to flood the internet of the likeness of certain pieces to missing relatives of onlookers. Initially these rumours had been the catalyst for various online horror stories and memes.

Side-by-side photographs of a young boy named Arnold Dent were posted on the web, alongside close-ups of Artwork number seven, which contained the striking likeness of the young boy. Dark skinned with a scar across his lower abdomen. Finally these rumours were taken seriously.

Readers will of course know the findings of investigations done by forensic analysts as well as the police. These findings can be found online in greater detail. To summarise, Julio Marquez was found guilty of abduction, murder, and desecration of a corpse, on all ten counts.

It is now widely known that the remains of these unfortunate people had been posed and encased in resin, which cut off any oxygen supply, which could have furthered any state of visual decay.

How long he had thought to get away with these crimes will never be known. Julio Marquez took his own life in his cell on the first night of his lifelong incarceration, with a bedsheet tied around his neck.

Photographs have attempted to be removed from social media platforms by lawyers of the effected families, as well as those overseeing such websites. Though these morbid images are still readily found, it is highly discouraged to continue sharing these images with others.

Shopping Centre

I make my way through dim, empty aisles to stand in the queue. I pick up a dusty bottle of moisturiser from a clearance shelf and place it into my shopping basket. The few working strip lights overhead stutter a few times before dying out with a ping.

I'm the only one shopping today. I lean against a bullet-torn checkout for a moment. I feel tired. It's quiet here, there's just the occasional zing of lost electricity in the air, and an odd moan from somewhere down the hall.

They sound like how I feel, having to shop for toiletries. I smile at the thought and feel the dry skin at the edges of my mouth crackle open. I haven't smiled in a while. Then I remember what happened before.

Memories come and go. Being dead has that effect on a person, I suppose. Terror shoots through my brain as I remember. I am so very tired… Why am I lying on the ground? Bottles litter the floor just beyond my reach. Moisturiser… That's right, my skin has been dry lately, peeling even. That's why I came here.

I raise a hand to touch my lips, but they reach nothing. That's strange. I move my arm upwards and there I feel my fingers. That's my wedding ring. Only, my hand is coming at me from above my head instead of where it should, under my line of sight.

My fingertips feel hair and I grab at it, until the world tilts in a dizzying whirl, and I am left looking up at the stump of my neck from my own lap.

Well, *shit.*

My skin looks so dry, it really does. I wonder if this place sells any sellotape?

Muttropolis

Bottlecap

We named the battered looking greyhound "Bottlecap," because she was missing an eye, and the closed-over wound somehow resembled the ridged edges of a bottle cap.

There were many dogs in the rescue home. Small dogs, fat ones, morbidly obese ones. Bottlecap, a retired racing dog that had been abused, stood out from the rest. She had been facing the back wall of her pen with her dry nose touching up against the grimy beige barrier. Her remaining eye didn't work too well either, we learned. So to her, she might as well have been standing at a window, gazing outward.

My own new home was beautiful. Everything was settled into place and my new housemate, Eliza, also made it feel like a second home to her. Even so, something was still missing.

The pitter-patter of little feet.

Though not of the expected kind—we needed a dog in the house to complete our home. And so, Bottlecap moved in with a certificate from the rescue centre declaring her officially 'adopted.'

I am now hers.

Dear Mam

Dear mam,

I'm sorry about the sick stain on your new mat, but you must know by now that the canned beef in gravy doesn't agree with me. You usually buy the canned beef in jelly!

Also, I'd like to mention that the garden perimeter has been kept clear of feline invasion for a *whole* week now. You're welcome!

I'm all for belly scratches and ear rubs as a reward, but if you could please stretch to a packet of Bonios as well, I'd be super grateful!

My ABSOLUTE love for you is UNDYING, as always!

Your ever loyal, best-est friend in the whoooooooole world,

Scruffy.

Walk in Winter

A walk with my Westie in winter,
Is much more of a meander.
A slow and deliberate saunter,
As she snuffles along, smelling the stories.

Clawed limbs of barren oak creak overhead,
As she cavorts around their curled roots.
Nose a-twitch at new sensations.
Nonsensical to me, daily news for her.

The castle sits, a-slumber and dark.
A silver pathway snaking alongside,
As empty grey skies turn to pink,
While we move to follow it homeward.

The heavens begin to sulk,
Purple now and ready to weep.

Westie-tude

Westie-tude describes my little
Dog that's full of beans.
Brave and bold and playful,
She is all the word can mean.

She snorkels snout-first through
The grass, sneakily serpentine.
She squiggles, and she slithers,
And her face is now stained green.

She bolts along behind the birds,
Most brazen and so brave.
Chasing after crows each day is,
A challenge she most craves.

Late at night she nuzzles,
And noses herself in near.
She snorts and snores so loudly,
Her sleep, the whole house hears.

Sun coming up or sun going down,
She is loyal at my side.
My dog, I so delight in,
My precious pet–my pride.

The Hereafter

Under My Bed

I hold hands with the monster under my bed.

It all started when I was a child. When my older sister, Catherine, woke me from my sleep with her loud crying as she sobbed into her pillow. Annoyed, I punched my head into my own pillow and turned to her.

"What's wrong now?"

I expected the usual cries of, "I miss Alex, when is Alex coming home?" Alex, our older brother, had gone missing.

This tore our family apart. Mam and Dad fought all the time until one day, Mam left. No goodbyes, just a messed-up bedroom and a missing passport. Dad started drinking a lot after that. The constant 'sightings' of Alex that turned out to be dead-ends, and heavy pressure from the police to remember *something*, anything else about that night; it drove him to find temporary peace at the bottom of a bottle.

When he disappeared, it had been at the end of a moody, storm wracked weekend. And Alex loved storms. The police surmised that Mam had left the front door open after coming in late from work, and that Alex had gone outside to see the lightning illuminate the late-night sky.

Back to my sister, whose sobs were muffled under the duvet which she had thrown over her head.

"What?" I sat up in the bed in my agitation. She did this multiple times a night, so all I remember wanting was an hour or two of uninterrupted sleep.

"Monster… Under your bed, Julie. Its eyes are glowing green."

I flipped my gaze to the ceiling, then leaned forward to look. I saw only the usual congregation of dust, odd socks, and broken toys. Nothing more. "Look, there's nothing there."

She peeped out from under the protection of the bedding. The look on her face, intensified by a sliver of moonlight through the slit in our curtain, frightened me too. The distress in her features made me feel like my blood was hardening inside of my veins.

"Nothing?" She asked. I nodded. She took a deep breath then lay back down. Her sobs dissolved to sniffles as she fell back asleep. I found myself lying there in my bed, wide awake. No matter how much I tossed, turned, or plumped up my pillow, I couldn't find rest until an eventual doze fell over me.

That's when a warm hand wrung its fingers through mine. Thinking it to be that of my sister, I fell asleep feeling comforted.

• •

The next night, my sister did not wake from nightmares. I awoke the following morning with my arm hanging over the side of the bed, towards the floor. Strange. Even stranger, the same thing happened the next morning and the next, until a week had passed.

No nightmares from Catherine, and always, I woke with my arm slung over the edge of the bed, towards the floor.

Curious, I planned to stay awake one night. I managed this and at around one o'clock, sure enough, the small, warm hand took mine in its grip. Moving slow, I peered down over the edge of my bed to see an odd, green-tinged hand linked with my own from under the bed.

One would think that in that situation, they would yank their hand away, scream, or yell. For me, there was only a feeling of calm. Peace. I closed my eyes, and in the morning awoke once again with my arm in the same position.

About ten years have passed since this started. I live on my own now, yet somehow, he has followed me here. The hand has aged over the years, just like my own. Now it's much larger than mine, though its grip is always gentle.

We never did find out what happened to our dear brother, Alex.

Ghost Town

When you think of a ghost town, it's all spectres that look like bed sheets haunting dark alleyways.

In truth, a ghost town isn't too different from a living one. Most of us are regular people doing regular jobs. Mine, for example, is cleaning up dog poo. Yep. Ethereal dogs and cats poop just as much as when they were alive.

I was a felon in life. When people like me pass on, we're 'tainted.' So, we get the shit jobs. Literally. I mean, I love dogs. It's just that being a spectral pooper-scooper for the rest of eternity is not what you would call 'Heavenly.' Still, at least I've not been sent to work downstairs. I guess only those who really hurt people in life have to work down in the spirit mines. All I ever did was skim some extra cash for myself on deals in the antiques showrooms.

I'm seeing a new guy now; he works up in the *people* department. He says that if I keep out of trouble and work another few decades without complaint, I might get promoted for good behaviour.

Jeez, though. These dogs sure do shit a lot.

Haunted Hearse

As I boarded a boat to go on a fishing trip, I died. Stupid, right? My ankle twisted as I stepped into the craft, I fell backwards and smacked my head on the old pier. That was that.

I figured it out right away, really. It wasn't hard to guess that I was dead, watching the crowd gather around trying to save my body. That, and the guy dressed in white that appeared next to me holding a harp. He was a dead giveaway, excuse the pun.

Turns out, I'm not quite ready to pass through the pearly gates yet. Gabriel, or Gabby as I've started calling him, told me that to make up for a bunch of crimes I did in my younger days, I need to *earn* my passage. I mean I wasn't a gangster or anything, I never hurt anybody. I used to steal stuff, stupid things like jewellery and the odd car to race around the country roads in.

You're probably wondering what I'm doing sitting in the passenger seat of a hearse right now. Gabby told me that if I help enough lost souls move on towards the light, then I'll earn my entry to Heaven. It didn't take me too long to figure out that lots of people follow their earthly remains around. So, I hang out with Earl the undertaker.

He doesn't know I'm here of course, but he plays good music when there aren't bodies on board, and I can at least enjoy the smell of his cigarettes. Though I can't smoke them myself.

Gabby, or maybe I should start calling him *Gobby* because the dude talks for days, shows up every so often to tell me I'm 'doing a great job, it won't be much longer now.' This last burial today, I count that as my seventy-fifth spirit sent onwards. You can see, I've been here for a while.

What about the other lost souls, you're probably wondering right? Well, Angels are pretty busy, being celestial beings and all, so they can't come on down to earth every time someone pops their clogs. So, they 'hire' dumb assholes like me with sins to work off, to do most of the meet and greets for them. Often these people are hanging around their bodies, crying and bawling and freaking out because nobody can hear them. Some of them have watched their own autopsies, and you can imagine how traumatised those poor bastards are. I try to calm them down, tell them I don't have the answers they are looking for but that big bright light they can see in the distance, well they need to head towards it.

It's nice when they move on, they often smile down at me as the light beams them onwards. Some of them are angry with their fate until they reach the light, so I figure once you step in there all your problems melt away. Nice for some.

I don't think Earl has much time left on this earthly plane either, by the sounds of him. He's been coughing bloody little bits into tissues.

And when he thinks nobody is looking, he's popping painkillers like they were smarties.

Be funny though, when he dies and 'ta-da,' here I am. Resident hearse-stalker here to show you the light, friend! I've got to amuse myself somehow, right? Haunting a hearse can be boring, but it's a living.

Excuse the pun.

So, this is Christmas

The Babóg

(Previously published in The Hollybough 2023)

Drowsy eyes which fluttered open under thick black lashes when you sat her up. I remember her eyes the best, those shocking blue irises sculpted with a windmill pattern. They were full of life, to me.

We called her the Babóg, though I'm sure when she came off the factory line in the 40's, she arrived with a proper name on her box. She was my nana's Babóg really. But my mother used to play with her, and when my sister Melissa and I came along, we took our own turns looking after the 'baby.'

She had a fully-rooted head of thick blonde hair, cut short like the fashion of the time. A little crocheted outfit, blue and white triangles, were the only clothing I ever remember her wearing. My nana fondly told of a time when the Babóg sported plastic shoes, a pretty pink dress and even a little bottle to drink from.

Which brings me back to the present. My hospital room is pale, though not in a drab sort of way. Rare winter sunlight streams in across the floor, and I'm certain that particles of dust flitter about in its rays. My eyes can't see quite so well now, but I am sure they must be there, cavorting around.

Most of my fluid intake is taken care of through the drip in my arm these days—but I do take some water at times, when one of the nurses sits and holds the glass steady for me. To them, I am like the Babóg. Though my own skin is not pristine moulded plastic but pale from illness, and my eyes are a muted brown.

My sister will be here soon, I overhear, knowing that this next visit will likely be the last. I feel a great sadness for her, sure that today is Christmas eve. I hear the crackling tinkle of Christmas carols on the nurse's radio at night. They play it when they think everyone is asleep. There are no decorations here, but I know that the festive time approaches.

I can feel heavy bubbles within my chest when I breathe, the sickness trapped deep within my lungs. I cough and wheeze. I'm sure I must sound like an old steam train at times, chugging up the last mile of its track.

My mind rolls back in time again, to the Babóg. To the anger on my mother's face whenever she caught me playing, the doll huddled close to my chest as if by letting her go, my own heart would escape and thump away across the floor. My sister knew how much I loved the toy, often giving her to me when nobody was looking. Times are different now, but then…

"Happy Christmas." There she is, my sister, looking pale and weary. She struggles to sit down next to me, her pregnancy well advanced now. She takes my hand in hers which to my surprise is warm. "I hope they're feeding you well here…"

Her smirk brightens up her face, mischievous as she points to the full bottle of fluid hanging above me. I try to reply but lose my breath to the lumbering malice in my chest which pinches off my air. She pats my shoulder when my head stills on the pillow.

"I know, you're dying to have some turkey and stuffing for dinner." She looks away, wiping a tear from her eye with her sleeve, pretending to sneeze into her sleeve instead. I point up at her hat, a woolly abomination shaped like a Christmas pudding, and she smiles again. "I thought you'd like that, alright."

I'm sure I drift off a few times, waking to the sound of her voice as she tells all the news from home. It's getting colder, and she pulls my blanket up closer over my chin. "I have something for you," she says, her voice husky with grief as she leans away out of view. She waits until my coughing stops and dries the corner of my eyes with some tissue. "Would you like your Christmas present now?" Even if I could have answered, she already has a brown paper bag up on the bed near me and is rattling around inside of it. She looks to me, smiles, and pulls out her offering.

My eyes brim over with tears, joyous ones which she wipes away once the Babóg is nestled into my arms. Like an infant just born, she is swaddled in a little yellow blanket, her eyelashes laying against plastic cheeks as she lays with me.

"I'm sorry she couldn't be with you until now." I hear her say, though I am lost in memories, a young boy again with scraped knees and a runny nose. Dim, as if very far away, I hear the vibrations of voices, and hold the Babóg tighter to my chest. "Nobody will ever take her away from you again, Liam." My sisters sad voice cuts through the hum. "When my boy is born, he'll have his own Babóg to play with. I promise."

She takes my hand, and I grasp her and my Babóg close as a rush of thick, fluid warmth rolls over me. I think I can hear the hymnal chiming of bells somewhere far away as my vision fades, and I drift away from all the pain and suffering, towards my own Christmas miracle as I find peace.

The Hobbyhorse

(Previously published in the Hollybough 2020)

In the window of the dusty second-hand shop it stood, broken, and neglected. In its heyday, it had been a top-of-the-line Ayres children's hobbyhorse, placed upright on its wooden stand with graceful carved legs that were poised in a prancing pose.

Once, it had been a splendid toy. It was the pride of its master's toy room, and young Redmond's favourite possession in the entire world. It had been the catalyst for so many adventures when he sat proud atop its back. Their rocking to-and-fro would mimic an avid chase after imaginary bad guys, as Redmond pretended to be like the heroes his parents used to watch in the Western films on their black and white television.

The decades passed by, and Redmond's attention changed over the years from playtime adventures to time spent studying for school. All too soon, he moved away from home altogether to start a family of his own. He had been an only child. Once his ageing parents sold the family estate to buy a smaller house near town, the hobbyhorse had been truly forgotten about. It was consigned to the attic many years before, to make room for more modern playthings and furniture as Redmond grew up.

It was a passive existence in the attic for all that ended up in storage, especially for the hobbyhorse. Fun times of play and movement made way to years of inactivity. This caused its wooden dowels and parts to stiffen and meld into place. Its racing years were over, for no longer could it bob and weave along in play.

•••

One bright spring day, everything changed. Light cut through the slumbering darkness of the attic like a razor for the first time in many years. Strange new people infiltrated the rooms silence. Coarse voices and modern flashlights danced their beams of light around the dark space in intrusive arcs.

Box by box and bag by bag, the contents of the attic had been removed. This upheaval caused a haze of dust to rise and swirl in lazy circles around the enclosed space on gushes of fresh air from below. The hobbyhorse was found after a few days, and with not-so-careful handling it had been dragged and pulled through the tight opening of the attic and into the glaring light of day. It lost its entire right ear in the process.

It was a sad sight to witness, as any trace of its former beauty was long faded and gone. It had once been a bright white in colour, with grey circular designs painted on the rear end and legs in a speckled pattern. It had been painted with an expression of joy by the craftsman that created it. A sparkle gleamed from well-polished glass eyes, which were a warm amber colour. The paint of its face and delicate eyelashes was now chipped. In some places it was all gone, giving the toy a bland, expressionless look.

The body's beautiful pale paintwork and the layers of gesso underneath were lost in some places, revealing the bare wood beneath from which it had once been carved and assembled with such care. Its once bright white mane made from real horses' hair had fallen out in clumps over the years. And all that remained were pathetic strands here and there. The tail was in an even worse state, in that there was none of it left. Traces of it were strewn on the ground at the base, as most of it now served as lining for various rodents' nests throughout the empty house.

Adorned once with golden hued reins made from real leather and dressed in a leather trimmed saddle on top of a velvet blanket, it had been resplendent as the light through the playroom window gleamed on the gold paint. When the light shone in around it on bright mornings, it gave the hobbyhorse an ethereal appearance, as if it were a mystical creature from a fantastical land.

Now, a cheap paper sticker was stuck to the side of its face that read, "Twenty Euro." It was placed upon the window of the charity shop amidst displays of used clothing on mass-manufactured mannequins, piles of crockery in 'nearly complete' sets and a plethora of stuffed animals.

A giant stuffed panda sat astride its lithe frame almost comically, though the shop assistant had placed it there after careful deliberation in the hope of making the sad looking horse seem like an exciting item again in the eyes of any children that passed by.

It wasn't a child that had taken an interest in the horse, however, but a middle-aged woman named Beth.

It stood inside the window, like a dim and pathetic ghost of its former grandeur. Beth stopped mid-step on the footpath when she spotted it, as a feeling of absolute sympathy overwhelmed her. The wheels of her mind spun and turned as she entered the small shop. By the time that her twenty-euro note had been handed over and another sticker had been placed on its rear saying "sold," she had formulated a complete plan of action. That very evening Beth and her husband Jim returned to collect the toy, with their teenaged son along to help. This time, it was carried out and loaded into Jim's van in a much more careful manner than its previous journey. Once inside, Beth wrapped the head in a soft layer of bubble wrap to protect its fragile nose and prevent any further damage to its remaining ear.

The next place of rest had been in their shed, in the centre of its sawdust strewn floor. It was flanked on either side by a wooden bench, each overloaded with various tools and metal instruments.

It had taken another full week before Beth stepped back into the shed. She had spent most of the week trawling through restoration pages on the internet and watching videos on YouTube to make sure that what she planned to do was indeed correct.

First thing was first.

Beth had not wished to remove the horse's original layers of paint and gesso, but it was in such dire condition that huge portions of it were already missing, and more was chipping away with each light touch. It had taken a week for all of it to be removed. It had all been rubbed away using rasps, sanders and eventually sandpaper until the horse lay on its side atop one of the timber benches with its wood exposed and clean for the first time in decades.

Jim helped Beth by removing the horse from its wooden stand. Beth stripped this back as well, delighting in the fact that the wood underneath appeared to have retained its quality over the years. There were no signs of woodworms, and no cracks or fissures near the joints. They were able to re-attach the hobbyhorse to it without issue.

To create a new ear to replace the one lost, Beth glued a small block of wood to the horse's head where the ear had been knocked away, using a strong wood glue. She carved it from there to be an exact match to the existing ear. After painstaking, patient work, both ears were a clever match for each other and made the horse's head complete again.

A fresh batch of gesso was mixed up, consisting of rabbit's skin glue and gilders whiting, which had to be applied while warm. Each coat on the horse had taken a week or more to dry, with a total of ten coats being applied.

The weather outside began to change from balmy sunshine to bleaker autumn conditions, and still the hobbyhorse stood sentinel in the shed as each coat of gesso dried. Once dry, Beth sanded it down, which gave the toy an overall appearance of being made from a fine porcelain. The same could not be said for Beth's hands, which were dry and sore from scrubbing and scraping at the wood for hours at a time.

To earn some extra pocket money, their son Sam painted a very light blue-grey colour to the body, which gave it a slightly off-white sheen. After four coats of the glossy acrylic paint had been applied, the old hobbyhorse looked bright and fresh. Using a special sponge, Beth created a dappled effect of bright white spots surrounded by dark grey spots in a hexagonal pattern around the toy's hindquarters, legs, and shoulders.

Wintertime approached as Beth awaited a special package from the USA which turned up one drizzly morning in mid-November. Inside the large box were pre-assembled hairpieces that she had ordered online, which had been fashioned using real horses' hair. Jet black, there was a complete tail, a thick mane set on a hide base and a separate forelock. Once the horse's glass eyes had been polished, and Beth had painted delicate lips and eyelashes to the face, the hairpieces were glued on. The toys features were now framed by long, elegant locks.

At the bottom of the large package sat ornate golden reins and saddle, with a green felt blanket for underneath the saddle. Once these had been tacked on to the rocking horse and polished, it was an inspiring sight.

Beth applied one coat of special wax to make the toy shine. After one final wipe of its eyes with a special cleanser used to polish glass, it was shrouded under a large canvas sheet. Hidden from the world once more, it was lifted with care into the back of their van and taken on what would be its final journey.

Amidst a chorus of energetic music and clamouring voices, the toy was set down. Jim removed its cover and a quiet hush dropped over those gathered. Colourful Christmas decorations were hung around the large hospital playroom. A group of twelve excited young children sat in a semi-circle around a tall, plastic Christmas tree.

"Hoorah!" They squeaked with unanimous delight, moving as fast as they could to clamour around and stroke the hobbyhorse's beautiful mane and touch its polished face.

"Thank you so much for this wonderful donation to the hospital" the matron said to Beth between bites of Christmas cake. They stood to the side of the play area with paper plates filled with cake and other festive holiday treats. Watching as the children each took turns to sit atop the horse and rock to-and-fro. A different type of glow surrounded the toy as the children played. It was a glow created by laughter and happiness.

"It was my pleasure. Now it will always have the love from children that it deserves." Never again would mice make nests from its hair or would the dust settle deep into the crevices of its eyes, dulling them to the world around it.

Love would encompass it, forever.

Bonus Content

Here follows the first chapter from my upcoming debut novel, a contemporary fairytale/horror story based in Southern Ireland, edited by Eamon at Clearview Editing.

I hope you enjoy this taster of...

Alderwood House

CHAPTER ONE

Joe stumbled up the cracked steps, the hood of his plastic poncho almost covering his face, its bright yellow a stark contrast to the gloom around him. The evening bells of the nearest church tolled their lonesome song as he paused, overlooking the ancient tombstones hidden among brambles and overgrown trees. He took a deep breath and made his way further into the graveyard, using his metal dinner fork to swipe nettles out of his way, stopping after a few paces to rest a shaky hand on a time-warped stone. With his hip against it, he did a slow count to five until his breathing slowed and his heart stopped trying to thump out through his ribs, his gaze darting in every direction for signs of movement.

A loud sound in the dried-up grass behind him had him twisting around, and his eyes widened as a darkness loomed over him.

"W-wait…" he stuttered, holding up the metal fork as a makeshift weapon but, in his panic, he stumbled backwards along the edge of an old stone. The leg of his trousers snagged on a grave marker, causing him to twist into an inevitable fall, landing with a thump against the headstone. He shrank into a foetal position as the shadow coated him, save for one sliver of light that gleamed like a dagger across his wide, terrified eyes.

"Please, you don't understand! I didn't mean to…" He clenched his eyes shut as he pulled himself into a tighter ball, waiting for whatever was to come next.

"Cut!"

Joe sat up and looked at Denise slipping the cover over the lens. She lowered the battered video camera to her side before giving him an appreciative thumbs-up with her free hand, her wrist rattling with plastic bracelets that had the names of current bands written on them in bold, bright letters.

The hood of his poncho had bunched up around his neck during the fall. Grinning, he pulled it back into its rightful place, then pointed the fork at his friend. She flicked her brunette ponytail behind her shoulder.

"I still don't get why I have to have a fork as my weapon," he said as she grasped him under the elbow and pulled him up in a smooth movement.

"It's supposed to be ironic, remember?" She let go of his arm and sat up on the nearby slab of long rock they used as a seat whenever they came here. "We need to get more footage of the tombstones, and some shots with those gnarled roots and stuff would look cool in the background."

"Tell me again why we're doing this?" He smoothed the poncho down around his sides, then sat next to her, its cheap plastic rustling in the silence of the graveyard.

"Because we're bored, it's nearly Halloween, and we have a video camera! Now, if we..." She trailed off, clicking the cap on and off the camera lens, something she often did while deep in thought.

A noise further ahead and to their left caused her to look up from her musings and cock her head sideways.

"Did you hear that?" she whispered, tugging the hood of her black jacket closer around her neck.

"It's just rats or something," Joe said. "It *is* a graveyard, after all." He inhaled the over-sweet smell of fruity toffees he'd taken from his pants' pocket, hoping to find his preferred flavour –cherry.

The graveyard had become a favourite hangout for the two teens over the last few months, as the boredom of living at Alderwood House fuelled their desire to explore further afield. That, and a mutual dislike of its new guardian. This pushed the two loners together and out into the overgrown lands around the property. They used these adventures to create fantastical stories that let them escape from their real lives as often as possible.

They first stumbled across this place on one of their trips down some steep, slippery hills way out back of the home. It was a wild place and most of the townsfolk thought it was too dangerous and unsuitable for a children's residential home, especially after the previous owners, Steve and Maria Harper, had that terrible accident. Both were well-liked in the town and were firm believers that children needed to get dirty and be a part of nature to learn anything about it.

This philosophy probably led to their demise, when they seemingly fell from a steep cliff deep in the woods. Many people in the town believed foul play was involved, for not only did the couple know the area well, they were also avid climbers.

No one could understand what brought the heavily pregnant young woman and her husband so deep into the woodland so late at night. To this day, it was a topic of deep speculation and rumour in the town.

The home had seen several new faces come and go since that time. Its newest addition was a cranky woman known to the few kids who remained as *Marjorie*. As far as they were concerned, she harboured a clear dislike for children.

Most of the land was now closed off, with barricades and long lengths of tattered plastic tape, and though they weren't really 'allowed' to explore the grounds, Joe and Denise disliked Marjorie so much that, whenever she wasn't looking, they pushed their way past the warped old barriers and made the place their own private kingdom.

A few nights earlier, Denise had come up with their latest movie idea. This time she would play an evil murderer and Joe the hapless victim. He grinned to himself as he chewed his cherry sweet, thinking back on all the crazy roles he'd played in their amateur horror movies to date: an evil puppet; an undead Geisha, and many more. You name it, Denise would make a story up for it in a heartbeat.

"There's definitely something here, though. I really don't think rats would make that much noise…"

Joe hopped down and strode towards the waist-high overgrowth that covered most of the cemetery. He was about to turn back and make fun of Denise for being such a scaredy-cat when he stopped himself, listening with more focus this time. Something was out there.

Denise gasped and he turned in time to see her run towards him, the camera gripped to her chest with both hands, her knuckles white. Her eyes were wide, her face pale.

"What's up?" he asked.

"Something… moved," she whispered, looking around, and he was sure he felt her tremble. "I don't like this, Joe. Let's head back…"

He, instead, stepped forward through the tight tangle of branches, until he was sure she couldn't see him.

"Hey, don't leave me here, Joe!" she cried.

He stifled a giggle as he watched her follow him, her long hair brushing off loose hanging leaves as she elbowed her way towards him in near-panic. They moved on together and soon found themselves standing at the edge of a small clearing.

The grass within was neat and short, and beautiful wildflowers framed the edge of the area, still visible even in the dim evening light. Their surroundings were taking on an auburn hue as the light dimmed further, yet Joe could make something out in the centre of the space–the humped silhouette of a large mound of earth, coated in a dense thicket of vicious barbed bushes and briers.

Through the impenetrable undergrowth, the decayed remains of a wooden building could be seen–an odd, circular structure sitting atop the mound of earth. This proved too intriguing to ignore and they continued on. The base of the mound was peppered with clusters of orange-coloured toadstools of various sizes and shapes.

"We've found a fairy fort!" Joe exclaimed as Denise caught her breath. Despite their earlier scare and the quick-setting sun, they smiled at each other before starting to explore. Joe circled his way around the structure, trying to figure out where the doors and windows might be, though he found nothing.

"Evil Fairies," Denise said, prodding a toadstool with the toe of her sneaker, her camera on her shoulder. "That would make a great horror movie–even better than the one we're working on now!"

Joe straightened to his full height, prepped for the shot as Denise uncapped her video camera and flicked the 'on' switch. Its small LCD screen glossed a blueish hue over her face as it hummed to life and she looked through the viewfinder.

"Ah, never mind," she said, lowering the camera to her side. "I can't see a thing through it, it's just too dark. We could come back tomorrow maybe…?" She let out a yelp and dropped the camera as she looked off to her left. It landed beyond the mushroom patch at her feet, settling into the thick grass at the base of the fort. Joe followed her frozen gaze, and goosebumps shot up across his shoulders at the sight of a hulking form emerging from the darkness at the trees' edge, creeping towards them.

He held his breath as the figure stepped forward into the brighter clearing, revealing itself to be a scruffy German Shepherd. The muscular dog padded its way closer to Denise, its amber eyes focused hard on her. Joe was full sure it was about to attack his stricken friend but, at the last moment, it continued past her and picked the camera up by the shoulder strap with its teeth, without touching it against any of the delicate toadstools. It turned and set it down at her feet, then placed itself between the two of them and the structure.

She scooped her camera up, glanced at Joe, and took a few slow steps back, the camera now around her neck.

"Nice dog…" Joe said with a dry-mouthed whisper as they took careful steps back to the edge of the clearing.

The dog's nose wrinkled up as it bared its teeth at them. Then it let out a most-horrifying snarl, spittle oozing from its jowls. It leaned back, its head lowered, never breaking eye-contact, growling deep in its throat. Then it lunged at them.

The teenagers spun and took off, crashing their way in a blind dash back through the dark woods towards the home. Joe nearly fell but Denise's grip kept him up, and they continued running, right through the graveyard and out the other side.

* * *

The dog went no further than the edge of the clearing. It continued to bark and snarl until no other sounds could be heard from the intruders. It tracked back inside and settled on the grass between the mound and the opening. With its head resting on its paws, it watched the mound, and waited.

Acknowledgements

My first massive thank you is for *you*, kind reader, for taking the time out of your day to read some of my work. I am truly humbled.

To my parents, Robert and Kathleen Foley. I will always be grateful to you both for not only the great support you give, but for putting up with my ideas for adventures over the years. Sure, we've had great craic!

To my husband, Eoin, whose support and understanding when I need to disappear at random times to 'let the stories out' is cherished, as are you. J'adore!

To my local writing group, The Mallow Scribes, based in Mallow Library. A massive thank you to the library staff, and as for the Scribes. I owe you all so much! The time we spend chatting over coffee and biscuits each week, testing out our ideas and stories is time very well spent, with real friends. You have shown me that writing does not have to be a lonely endeavour.

Suspicious of Scones, you know who you are, and will always have my friendship, love, and suspicious nature of random baked goods…

To Denyse Woods, an extraordinary writer and tutor, I am beyond thankful. Your creative writing courses have taught me *so* much. You helped me to learn to believe in myself and got me started with submitting my work out into the big wild world.

To Eamon of Clearview Editing, whose editing skills can be seen in the Alderwood House teaser, goes my eternal gratitude and awe. To Keidi and the team at Your Book Angel goes my absolute appreciation, thank you for helping me to put this collection together. You've been wonderful to work with.

Thanks to those working at The Mallow Star for supporting all of the Scribes, by publishing our stories and poems each week. We appreciate it very much.

I thank all members of the Mallow Arts Festival committee for the work every single one of you puts into supporting the arts in our town, and to each other, you are all inspiring and amazing people.

To my dog and cat… Muahaha! No, that's the end now, I promise.

Go raibh míle maith agat!

Milton Keynes UK
Ingram Content Group UK Ltd.
UKHW012228180624
444315UK00001B/204